Weathering Life

Jacqueline Nathan

BookLeaf Publishing

Weathering Life © 2023 Jacqueline Nathan

All rights reserved.

No part of this publication may be reproduced, stored in a retrieval system, or transmitted, in any form or by any means, electronic, mechanical, photocopying, recording, or otherwise, without the prior written permission of the presenters.

Jacqueline Nathan asserts the moral right to be identified as the author of this work.

Presentation by *BookLeaf Publishing*

Web: www.bookleafpub.com

E-mail: info@bookleafpub.com

ISBN: 9789357441940

First edition 2023

To my grandmother, Mary Louise Stewart Batiste, who taught me how to get my mind right; in order to deal with life.

ACKNOWLEDGEMENT

I want to thank my daughter, Ashley, for suggesting I "put it all on paper" to share some of my humor, and insight with others. Thank you to my sister Andrea, for letting me use her as a sounding board, and to my Aunts LaVerne and Floristene for keeping me on task.

PREFACE

I was the kid that clowned, and always had a joke or a rhyme. I fell in love with literature, and later became passionate about writing; especially, poetry. This collection of poems was either written individually or formulated from short stories I've written.

True Labor

The nesting period has begun
And all preparations shall soon be done
There is room in my home and my heart too
As I envision a place for you

Although pain and time is what I must bare
This is a moment in which you will share
But in pain there is worth
For out of my labor shall come your birth

But true labor has yet begun
After all of these tasks have been done
As my time draws near
I know that you shall soon be here

As a family we shall be as one
And so true labor has yet begun

Advice To The Groom

Train your hands not to touch
Teach your heart to not lust
Keep your feet from running the street
And only wink at your wife
That is my strong advice

True Reflections

I look in the mirror and what do I see
A reflection
But is it really me
I can see what's on the outside, but not within
For my inner self is where the true reflection
begins
I searched myself to try and see
Without this physical image, just what would I
be
Does my true personality show in any way
How do I conduct myself from day to day

I wonder what you would conclude
If you could view my attitude
And so, not only this but am I biased or
prejudiced
Do I have any sort, of evil or rage within my
heart
Now that I've taken an inside view
Won't you look inside of you
Outer beauty is nice to behold
But without inner beauty
There beats no heart of gold

Broken

Lost
Engulfed
Swallowed up from within
With broken dreams
And shattered scenes
And a heart that just won't mend
Time, so said
Can heal a broken heart
How much time then, does it take
To mend the heart that's torn apart

The Struggle Is Real

Yes I'm young, but I feel pressure too
How do I keep on going, with what I'm going
through
Pressured by my peers
Stereotyped by man
Victimized by the police
Bullied by my enemies
The temptations of the streets
Social media spinning satan's truth,
Promiscuity, pornography, vanity, and lies
Spreading rumors and ruining young lives

How do I keep on going
When I don't know if I can make it through
Nothing is working out
Everything is going wrong, GOD there's so
much going on
I feel as though I'm losing my grip
My dreams and my thoughts are all adrift
I'm kneeling here in despair, living in a world
that seems not to care
Sometimes I feel like I'm out here all alone
Fighting the good fight, but yet alone

I need you, Lord, to help me carry on

Reach down and heal my wounded heart
Whisper in my ear
It's your voice I need to hear
Nourish my weary soul, renew my strength
Restore my praise and let me rejoice
Lord, I NEED to hear your voice

Help me establish a better prayer life
Send me the right friends to help me in this fight
Cover me with your blood every day
Protect me from dangers I can and cannot see
Lord, DESTROY my enemy
Ah yes, there it is, the warmth of your love
caressing me
As your grace and mercy surround me
Giving me the strength to fight this fight
Letting me know that everything is going to be
alright

It's No Secret

A secret told in confidence
A secret I told to my confidant
A secret told, a secret kept
Your secret she said
Will never leave my lips
A secret told was not kept
A secret is not a secret when
Your confidant can't
Keep her big mouth shut

The Priest Got Jokes

Stuck between a rock and hard place you say
Someone said good morning and you cursed the
day
Does it seem as though your back is up against a
wall
Well with my luck it'll probably fall
So there's no reason to pretend that everything's
okay
Hell - if it weren't for bad luck, nothing would
go my way
I visited a priest to sit and discuss
My feelings of rage, anguish, and disgust
My son, he said, you must try to make things
work
Even though it does seem as though you're a jerk
But Father I cried, there's no reason to pretend
I feel that my life will soon end
My son he said, if such is the case
Do you mind if we discuss your bones' resting
place

It's Okay

It's okay
If you dream of reaching the moon
But fall among the stars
If you reach and then fall
It's better than not trying at all

It's okay
If you have to dream a new dream
Or start over again
Hold on tight and try not to fret
Allow yourself to breathe
Because this is not the end

When We Argue

When we argue, and I hope we never do
Don't yell and scream at me, and I'll do the same
for you
Because if we do
You won't hear me and I won't hear you
Don't insult me or call me names
Let's just deal with the situation at hand

Please don't ever, I mean never, be so mean
As to throw anything at me
Shove me, hit me, or put your hand in my face
When we argue let's maintain
At least six feet of personal space

My hearing is fine, so don't move in too close
Don't do anything to make me feel threatened or
provoked
Remember that we love each other, no matter
how we're feeling right now
Let's just agree that we disagree, and discuss this
at some other time or place

I'm Here For You

Whenever you feel you need a friend
I want you to know that I'm here
If only to lend a listening ear
Or dry a single tear
Whatever you feel or want to share
I promise that I will always be there
Simply because I care

Hang In There

I feel that I have so much to give
And countless reasons why I should persevere
There were times when I was so depressed
I saw my life as being useless
With seemingly no reason for my existence
It's then that I almost lost all resistance
I don't know how these thoughts filled my head
But they somehow managed to seep in
And it wasn't always easy to control them
From then on it was almost as if
I was obsessed with becoming self-destructive

I feared one day that it would be told
How someone found my body lying cold
Not so much the fact that I was dead
But how and why it occurred instead
Because I was too afraid or ashamed to seek
help
Only thinking of myself
Not caring about anyone or anything else
I found out that nothing is as it seems
And evil lurks behind the scenes
Dare to hang in there and you'll see
Just how strong you can be

The Rock

13

How does a rock stand strong and tall, when it's
becoming worn and small
How does what time has eroded, be restored
So now the rock begins to roll
Continuously on the move
No place to rest, no time to stop
Unless something changes its path
Perhaps it did not roll aimlessly
Maybe now its where it should be
The chiseler found it, worn and frail
He chiseled, filed, hammered, and sawed
Until that worn down rock, became a work of art
That rock went beyond being restored
Tis now better than it was before

Not for Naught

Rise up my children
Wipe the sleep from your eyes
Greet the new day
For God has Blessed the sunrise
Do you see the roads our ancestors paved
You are the framework for all that was made
When the construction of walls, halls, and
corridors
Buildings to which we were denied access
Were built by us, but not for us
For our kind was not allowed

Welcome to the new day
Ushered in by blood, sweat, and our ancestors'
death
Within these walls, you can now dwell
So learn your lessons, and know them well
They not only built but also fought
Now you prove that all was not for naught

Questions

Is it always darkest before dawn?
Is it true that you sometimes stand alone?
Does every cloud have a silver lining?
Are brighter days ahead?
If I do good, shouldn't goodness follow me?
Where is the light at the end of the tunnel?
Am I in control of my destiny?
Or am I running the course set for me?
Am I destined in life to fail?
Should I grab the bull by the horn?
Or swing him by the tail?

I Weep

When the dark things of the world make their
way front and center
This is when the tears begin to flow
Like giant raindrops bearing splinters, they can
no longer be contained
I weep for those whose blood paints our streets
No comfort, no peace, and there seems to be no
relief
for these senseless killings that should not be
Babes killed while still in the womb
Children snatched from this world much too
soon
I weep for our youth taking their own lives
Believing non-truths due to ill spouted lies
I've heard people say, suicide is a coward's way
But that's not really true
Taking your own life is a hard thing to do
And it should never be done
Suicide comes from a spirit of destruction
Don't let anything or anyone push you to the
edge
So before you step out on a ledge, or pick up a
gun and put it to your head,
or drown yourself out of this world whether by
liquid or pill

These are the dark forces trying to subdue your
will
Step back, breathe, what's one more day to find
your way

Life can Be A Mess

I stood in front of my class today
My appearance was that of a clown
Not dressed up, but dressed down
To teach them some things they should know
Educate them on situations as they grow
Teach they said, why are you dressed that way
Did you forget to do your laundry
That's when I began to explain
You may say that I look a mess
But living gets hard, and life becomes messy
sometimes
This yellow tie represents joy and sunshine
When I see yellow this is what it brings to mind
Sometimes a depressed mood is indicative of
what's called the blues
Hence the blue shoes
Are you seeing my red shirt, so bold and bright
When one becomes angry, you're said to be
seeing red
How about my black pants
What do you think they represent
Those are the dark days that arise in life, pain,
death, heartache, and grief
No matter what you wear or how you dress
Remember that life can be a mess

Special Delivery

Dear God,

When they're at school, work, or busy with play
Lord, protect our children every day
Cover them with your blood, I plead
Hide them from the enemy
Forgive them, Lord, when they're led astray
Send your angel to show them the right way.
Amen

Sincerely
A mother's heart

This Little Ring

I found a ring on the ground one day
At a time when I was feeling blue
I picked it up and studied it carefully
And it reminded me, of myself
This little ring, that I found, lying on the ground
With its band bent somewhat out of shape, its
circle now imperfect
Its gold tarnished, scuffed, and scratched
The diamond undaunted, and still intact, in the
center of its band
The brilliance lost, that it once knew
Tis the way I was feeling too, bent out of shape,
and somewhat blue
A little tarnished and worn down, without much
of a shine
As I held the ring, I knew, it wasn't as bad as it
seemed
In a skilled jeweler's hand, it would be as good
as new
The band hammered, to restore, its perfectly
rounded shape
The scratches and scuffs, grounded to smooth its
grooves and troughs
With the gold polished and the diamond buffed
to return its lustrous shine

This little ring that I found, lying on the ground,
reminded me of myself
I am intact but somewhat scuffed, and a little
bent out of shape
But in the Master craftsmen's hands
He polishes and restores me to the brilliance that
he sees
Who would have thought that it would speak to
me
Without making a single sound
This little ring, that I found, lying on the ground

Lucious Luther

Lucious Luther
That's my man
In real life, a bronzed statue, he would be
A handsome brother carved out just for me
Dark chocolate is my preference, and I love it
bittersweet
As long as my chocolate knows, he was created
just for me
Two strong, but gentle arms, and a finely
chiseled chest
With six-pack abs and a lot of swag, my Luther
knows me best
The sweetest lips with kisses honey dipped
His love free flowing, and always knowing
That he was meant for me
Lucious Luther, that's my man

When I'm Eighteen

Can't wait until I grow up and turn eighteen
So I can get out of here
My mom's always telling me what to do
I'm not allowed to have fun, until what she
wants is done
So what if I don't clean my room and play video
games all day
Why can't I do things my own way
"My house my rules" that's what parents always
say
It sounds so automated because I hear it
constantly
Pick up your clothes, take a bath, do your
homework, or you can't have that
It comes in one ear and goes out of the other
Parents always think that they know better
I'll ask to go to the movies, and I'm willing to bet
She'll ask me, "Have you cleaned your room
yet"
What does a clean room have to do with
anything
It's just another way to keep me in
Now I'm sitting around all day
My mom's taken my games away, and gone is
my phone too

What am I supposed to do

So I decided to go ahead and clean my room
Now this is the way I'd like it to stay
Everything's picked up and put away
And needless to say, my mom is so happy
It was nice to see that big old smile on her face
And I too was happy with my newfound space
It was as though I'd discovered my room for the
first time
I love my mom
And she knows what's best for me
She cooks my food, cleans my clothes, and
drives me constantly
and a little crazy too
She only wants the best for me, because that's
what moms do
There's no one else that will do, what a real mom
does for you

African Yes But American Too

Black, Negro, Colored
Whichever of these you may call me
But a nigger, no, that is not a name I answer to
If you knew what it really meant
You'd know it refers to you
African yes, but American too
And still a man, unlike you

We were counted as nothing because of the color
of our skin
And sold off as animals in a land to which we
were not akin
In the bible, David said, "I once was young but
now I'm old, and I've never seen the righteous
forsaken, nor his seed begging bread'.
Better days are coming, I know what lies ahead
You shall see in the days to come, God's
righteousness
And his will, will be done
Times are changing, just wait and see
Our children will change our history

You said that I, belong in a tree
Is that the reason that you hung me

Or is it because you could not take away, my
African pride or dignity
Did I hear say that we were lazy
No-no baby we were never lazy
This county was borne of our sweat, and built on
our backs
The overseers whip we will never forget

Our sons
The ones
To which you will stake no claim
The ones conceived and born in shame
These are our sons, born of my daughters
Whom you did violate
They will come and set the record straight

My son James, will sing it out strong and loud
Reminding our race to always be proud
My son Malcolm will refuse to take your name
Because it represents disgrace and shame
My son Martin, although his time won't be long
Will place all men as equals, as they belong
You thought you could silence him, but his
dream still lives on
African yes, but American too
And still a man, unlike you

www.ingramcontent.com/pod-product-compliance
Lightning Source LLC
LaVergne TN
LVHW021336200726
843509LV00014B/2547